The Mindfulness Workbook for Women

Simple Prompts to Find PEACE and PRESENCE in a Stressful World

LAUREN BROOK

Published by Sourcebooks
P.O. Box 4410, Naperville, Illinois 60567–4410
(630) 961-3900
sourcebooks.com

Printed and bound in the United States of America.
POD 10 9 8 7 6 5 4 3 2 1

Introduction

Transcendental meditation. Vipassana. Full-lotus, half-lotus. Loving-kindness and progressive relaxation. In the world of mindfulness, there are infinite options. And with infinite options comes just as many questions. Do you need to sit on the floor with your legs crossed to practice mindfulness? Or will deep breathing through a yoga practice suffice? Are you supposed to meditate every morning, every day, once a week? Does it take an hour, or will twenty minutes do? And what happens when you don't have twenty minutes every day to dedicate to your own mindfulness? What if you don't have five minutes? And what do you do when you don't even know where to start?

The world of meditation and mindfulness is full of misconceptions and variety. It is bursting with gurus, Zen masters, and variations. So, so many variations. And not everyone has the time to sit on the floor with perfect posture for three hours straight in the name of meditative wellness.

So, where do you start? Do you take a couple thousand-dollar Transcendental Meditation courses? Do you download a mindfulness app or audiobook? Memorize the traditional Vedic texts and mantras? Perhaps the Buddhist koans? Do you now need to know everything about karma and enlightenment? Do you need to go pick up a floor pillow and some yoga clothes?

There are many different methods, techniques, and paths for mindfulness. And you may want to explore a few of them on your journey. But for right now, this book is a starting place to connect to your day-to-day wellness. Using prompts, breathing exercises, and practices in relaxation and presence, *The Mindfulness Workbook for Women* will help you embrace your own self-care and start to feel the benefits of meditative mindfulness. In this book, you'll learn how to be present in the moment and counteract negative thought patterns. You'll learn how to consciously focus your attention and connect with your surroundings. You'll find better tools to relate to your body, your mind, and to others around you. You'll learn how to integrate simple meditation into your routine and revamp your overall wellness.

Just one minute a day, and you're on your way to a more peaceful, balanced life.

WHAT IS MINDFULNESS?

The tradition, practice, and teaching of meditation is *old*. Thousands of years old. And it has stood the test of time because of its mind, body, and overall wellness benefits. Practicing presence helps us counteract the stresses of our hectic lives. Think about it—our thoughts tend to follow specific patterns. The same input often produces similar output. So, we run through the same routines of thought day in and day out, stuck on autopilot. Mindfulness is a way to turn off that autopilot and connect in the moment.

Imagine waking up in a rush because you forgot to set your alarm. A simple mistake, but suddenly your entire day has derailed. On your way into work, you're cut off in traffic. And then you spill coffee on your shirt. Soon enough, these few events collapse on top of one another, and your brain slips into autopilot, moving down a familiar path toward a total bad mood.

Mindfulness helps you resist these careening brain paths. You'll still wake up late every once and a while and spill coffee on your shirt—that won't change. But you'll be able to quickly *move on* from those bad moments. Basically, mindfulness is all about awareness and perspective. It helps us understand that much of what causes us pain is external, and when you can disconnect from those outside influences, you can discover your own inner peace.

So how do we achieve mindfulness? Through practicing meditation and training our minds so they stop falling into those brain routines. The practice of meditation, at its core, is about paying gentle attention. We have to retrain our brains to disengage from the constant thoughts, fears, anxieties, day-to-day minutiae running through our minds at rapid speed and instead focus on the small details. We can focus on the moment, our surroundings, paying gentle attention to a certain feeling or idea. It's all about being present, which leads us to have a fresh, relaxed perspective on the world around us.

There are many ways to practice meditation. In this book, we'll explore just a few of the different methods, along with prompts to help guide you through your mindfulness journey.

The Benefits of Mindfulness

The benefits of mindfulness are many and varied. It's also important to note that mindfulness is not a blanket prescription to solve all of your problems. Rather, mindfulness is a tool that will better equip you to deal with your problems in a healthier, more productive manner. Here are some of the benefits of a dedicated mindfulness practice:

PERSPECTIVE

Remember those brain routines we were talking about in the last section? Perspective is what happens when we step out of autopilot and take stock of what's actually going on in our heads.

We do this by taking a step back and looking at all the thoughts and emotions in our brains. We don't judge these thoughts; we simply become aware of them. We lay them all out on the table and take stock of what's in front of us. Then, we discern which thoughts need our attention and which can be dismissed and move forward.

Imagine you are trying to move a canoe down a river. If you're a passenger in the boat, you can only see what's in your direct line of vision, and it is easy to get swept up in the current. However, if you're standing on the shore, you're able to take stock of the river and notice the potential roadblocks the canoe will face. You're able to see the debris in the water—the leaves, sticks, and eddies—and discern them from the actual problems—the logs and rapids blocking the canoe's passage. When you take stock of the whole situation, you're better able to direct the canoe safely down the stream.

This perspective, this stepping out of the stream, is one of the largest benefits of cultivating mindfulness. After practicing this shift enough times, it becomes easier to carry this perspective into other areas of our life. We can step back and acknowledge the truth of our situations.

STRESS REDUCTION

Believe it or not, some stress is good for us. Putting effort into a creative hobby or working to achieve a goal is a good form of stress, just like exercise is! Stress can push us to be our best selves, helping us develop necessary resilience and life skills. However, when not managed correctly, stress can also be a large health hazard.

What determines if stress is good or bad is often in how we relate to that stress. Are we choosing to have it, or is it being imposed on us? What type of control do we have over it? Do we have an actionable path forward? Do we feel personally powerful over that stress? Basically, what it boils down to is, *can we do something about it?*

We often see the words "attachment" and "suffering" when we read about meditation and mindfulness. Attachment is often cited as the root of all suffering, and to reduce human suffering we must reduce attachment.

Attachment in our modern context more accurately means "longing." It's important to understand that this very rarely relates just to objects or things. This attachment is the longing for circumstances to be different than they are. This is often the result of looking into the future or the past, as opposed to being in the present moment. "I wish I were rich" is a longing for your personal wealth to be different. "I wish people would behave differently" is another example of this attachment or longing for different circumstances. Longing is at the root of many of our negative stressors because, oftentimes, we can't do much about the situations our brains are attached to. There isn't an actionable plan, we ruminate in the wants and what-ifs, and that's how stress manifests.

Which is why mindfulness is a great tool to counteract negative stress. By being in the moment, mindfulness reduces our attachment and helps us manage our stress. When we are focused on the sensation of each breath, and feel our chest slowly lifting and falling, we are no longer ruminating on our longing, or the stress it might cause. Instead, we're focused in the now.

EMPATHY AND COMPASSION

One form of mindfulness is called loving-kindness meditation. This method of meditation focuses on feelings of care, tenderness, love, and compassion to cultivate empathy for yourself and those around you. Practicing this form of mindfulness helps you accept yourself, your faults, your failings, and your strengths, and love those around you in the same way. Loving-kindness knows no bounds—it's a practice of compassion that helps you empathize with strangers, friends, neighbors, family, and, most closely, with yourself. Sounds pretty positive, right?

Being more compassionate is a profound change that can have incredible effects on our lives very quickly. Often in our day-to-day lives, it's easy to fall into negative feelings toward yourself and others. Because of the stresses of our world, it's easy to let a bad mood affect how we treat our friends and loved ones, our neighbors and strangers, even unintentionally. When we're stressed, we begin to focus on those stressors, and we become less emotionally sensitive to the people that matter—it's falling into that autopilot again. Loving-kindness meditation helps us remain sensitive to others even during our own difficult and challenging times, and with increased empathy and compassion, we foster greater connection, altruism, and positivity in our lives.

FOCUS

Your ability to focus can be trained. Like a muscle in your arm, the more often you train it, the stronger that muscle gets. Focus is exactly the same, and mindfulness is the tool you can use to beef up your focus. Cultivating mindfulness requires you to exercise the brain and teach it new ways to focus.

One misconception of focus is that it requires you to push out all other thoughts and feelings. Many believe it to be a process of exclusion, pushing away external situations that aren't pertinent to your current focus. Often, it's more of a combative process, especially with particularly virulent thoughts! This is where mindfulness steps in. Recognizing our own thoughts should never be combative; we should simply note them and move on. Training the mind to acknowledge and accept thoughts, whether good or bad, and then move on from them allows us to have greater focus.

TEN TIPS TO BE MORE MINDFUL

1. **Meditate**

    The practice of meditation is at the core of living a mindful life. Mindfulness is a skill that can be developed;

practice will make you better! You will find that on some days being mindful will be incredibly difficult. Your mind will bombard you with thoughts, and it will be nearly impossible to simply concentrate on your breath and block out the rest. However, over time, meditation will get easier and will become the bedrock for your overall mindfulness.

2. **Don't rush**

Living a mindful life requires deliberate intention, and we build this intention day by day. It's a process—when we take things a little slower, it's easier to take accountability for your thoughts and emotions and lead a more mindful life. So slow down and don't rush the process.

3. **Notice your breath**

Our breath is a constant instrument of focus. Be attentive to it, pay it heed. When you catch yourself in a pattern of stress or negativity, take a few moments and focus instead on your breath. This method often serves as a great reset during a busy day.

4. **Chew slowly**

How often do you pay attention to the actual process of eating? How many times do you put the phone down, sit quietly, and nourish your body—paying particular attention to the food you have in front of you? We often eat in a distracted fashion. We take a bite, then scroll on a web page or watch TV. But what happens when we decide to be more present? Mindful eating is a great way to slow down and connect with the experience. Try to spend at least one meal a day chewing slowly. Put your phone down and actually taste the food you're eating!

5. Smell the roses

It's easy to dismiss the sounds, smells, and visuals of our daily routines—I mean, we see them every day! You wake up at the same time, brew the same coffee or tea, and take the same route to work. Often, we spend so much time with the same smells and sights that our brain begins to tune them out. Spend some time during your daily routine truly experiencing the world around you. Take a deep breath in the coffee shop and enjoy the scent of the beans roasting. Step outside and take a lungful of crisp, fresh air. What do you notice?

6. Don't watch the clock

In our modern lives, scheduling is imperative to get things done—they're impossible to do away with completely. However, sticking to a schedule can also provide a low level of anxiety throughout our days. We compulsively check clocks and our phones, always anticipating the next thing we have to do. The next meeting, the next task, the next meal. As much as you can, try to forget about the clock. Experience your current events; the future will come in due time. Enjoy the present. Let yourself be clock-free for a day.

7. **Express gratitude**

One of the most effective ways to combat attachment and suffering is to express gratitude. Being actively thankful for our gifts combats the incessant need for more. Spending even a few moments feeling grateful is a sure way to brighten an otherwise tough day. Spending time examining what we have or have accomplished is integral to living a mindful life.

8. **Do the chores**

There are tasks that have to be done that—guess what—aren't very fun. Whether it be laundry, balancing your budget, or schlepping around the grocery story, there are always going to be those chores that you hate doing. One way to make these tasks a bit more bearable is to do them deliberately! Use them as an excuse to practice mindfulness. Attend to the task at hand and be attentive to the process. What does freshly dried laundry smell like?

What are the textures of the fabrics between your fingers? What does the rhythm of folding clothes feel like? Paying attention in the moment will help us erase those negative thought patterns and find a new, productive way to conquer our least favorite chores.

9. **Forgive yourself**

Early on in our lives, we are taught how to forgive others for their wrongs. However, we aren't as trained in forgiving ourselves. Mindfulness is a skill that can help with this. You cannot and will not always be the best you can be. Some days will be easy, some days will be very hard—and that's all okay. Forgiving yourself for not being perfect is how you learn to lead a more present, empathetic, and kind life.

10. **Be playful**

Mindfulness thrives in novel experience. We are never more in the present moment than when we experience something new or different. Spend some time changing your schedule when you can. Small changes are best. Eat (slowly!) at a different place than your "usual." Take a different route to work and notice the different buildings or people you see on your journey. These novel experiences will help you stay in the present and disrupt your negative routines.

How to Use This Workbook

The Mindfulness Workbook for Women is broken into several sections of prompts, focusing on different pillars of your mindfulness journey. These prompts are designed to draw out your thoughts and experiences during your mindfulness practice and to facilitate your progress. Here are the subjects you can expect to see:

1. Mindfulness
2. Body Awareness
3. Meditation
4. Self-Love
5. Mindful Self-Care
6. Gratitude
7. Mindful Emotions
8. Mindful Relationships

While the exercises are meant to be simple, the journaling can take as much or as little time as you want. Even if it's simply one good breath or filling out your workbook and meditating for ten minutes, the hope is that *The Mindfulness Workbook for Women* will give you the tools you need to inject calm into your every day.

Start with one good breath. Breathe in through the nose and out through your mouth, exaggerating the breath. You may feel the rise and fall of the air in your chest, your stomach, your shoulders. Try this for sixty seconds. Where did you feel the breath moving? What noises did you hear while you were concentrating? Did anything interrupt your breathing?

Write down a few sentences detailing why you want to be mindful in your daily life. This will serve as a reminder as you start your mindfulness journey.

When was the last time you felt scattered or stressed?
Can you trace it back to a source? Free write about that
experience and what you believe caused your stress.

....

Take sixty seconds to center yourself. Search for your current emotional landscape. Are you anxious? Happy? Angry? Joyous? Remember that we shouldn't judge these emotions; we simply want to observe them. Write a list of all the things you felt during that sixty seconds. Are there any patterns?

What is your favorite emotion? It can be positive or negative. Remember, emotions are simply what you feel, not something to be judged! Write a few sentences describing your favorite emotion and how it serves you.

....

What is one of your favorite memories? Take a minute and relive that memory. Try to reconstruct the smells, sounds, and tactile experiences. How did you feel that day? Then, write down as much as you can recall. What did this memory bring back for you?

Take a break and visualize a tree in your mind with as much detail as you possibly can. Re-create the sight, the feel of the bark. What do you see and smell? How does this tree make you feel? Free write about this exercise. Was it difficult to visualize the details?

....

Get a bit of food or your favorite drink. Eat or drink it as slowly as you can. For sixty seconds, write down the details of this experience. How does the food feel in your hands, on your tongue? How does it taste? What does it smell like? How does your body respond? Get as much detail about the experience as you can down on paper.

Focus on your breath and erase your thoughts for sixty seconds. As your mind attempts to intrude, continue to focus on your breath and body. Was this difficult or easy today? What were the thoughts that stole your attention the most?

Once again, focus on your breath for one minute, but this time, try to find all the different places in which you can feel your breath as it moves in and out (stomach, chest, nose, etc.). Do you feel your breath in your cells? Can you picture that oxygen spreading to your fingers, through your bloodstream? List the different places below.

For a minute, visualize the face of your favorite person. Try to hear their voice and remember all the details you can. What are some of their most important characteristics? How do you feel with them held in your mind? If you could speak to them right now, what would you say?

Take sixty seconds and think of a difficult experience you've had. Try to divorce your emotions from this memory, and view it nonjudgmentally. Did the memory change? Was it difficult to remain unbiased? Try replaying it with the sound off, or in black and white. What did you learn?

Think of a word or phrase that's important to you. It can be a poem or a song lyric or just your favorite word. Spend a minute thinking of it; hear its rhythm and feel its meaning to you. As you repeat the word or phrase, does it lose its meaning or gain more?

What does presence mean to you? How have you demonstrated presence in the past day? Week?

Body Awareness

During your journey into the world of meditation and mindfulness, you'll see your body going through many changes. It's possible you'll notice spontaneous bursts of gratitude and happiness. You'll carry less tension in your shoulders and spine. Situations and events that previously may have triggered a cascade of negativity will have less sharpness to them. It becomes easier to simply shrug things off and move on from experiences that would have previously perturbed you. Your body is adapting to a new sense of forgiveness and peace.

The mind and the body are inextricably connected. Stress in our minds often exhibits itself in the body—we experience a quickened heartbeat, tight muscles, aches at our temples and sweaty palms. These feelings often go unheeded because we're so used to carrying our stress.

Overall, mindfulness will hopefully supply feelings of reduced stress and anxiety. When we begin to spend less time in our own heads, worried about the past and the future, we learn how to become more present, and that presence affects every aspect of our lives. You'll notice the physical difference in your body. You'll discover a sense of confidence and ease. You'll ditch the sweaty palms and achy brain and finally feel peace.

These changes will be fairly gradual. It takes practice and time before your mind begins to fall into mindful habits, and your body will follow. Just as our brains need to be trained to step outside of negative thought patterns, our bodies will need to learn to recognize tension and stress and create patterns for relief.

The prompts in the following section will focus on our mind's connection with our body, and how we relate to that connection.

NEW TECHNIQUE: BODY SCAN

Sit in a calm area where you will not be distracted. Take your first few deep breaths and close your eyes. Allow yourself a few moments to sink into your position. It's not necessary that your back is perfectly straight; instead, simply sit up as tall as you are comfortable. Feel the chair or floor beneath you; notice your feet and legs, and how they're positioned. Notice the space that your body is occupying as well as everything that it's touching. Feel the tactile sensation of your clothes and the chair or floor against you. Now you're ready for a body scan.

Start at the top of your head. Focus your awareness on

your head, your skull, your brain. Feel the emotional quality of your body there. Now continue to draw your attention down the length of your body, slowly shifting your focus to the different areas—your neck, your torso, your limbs. Notice the emotional quality of each area. Is there a tension anywhere? Are you feeling moments of discomfort or frustration? Where are those feelings hovering? Don't forget to check the little places as well—think about your veins, your fingers, your nose, ears, toes.

Remember, these exercises are nonjudgmental; we're not judging any part of our body or how it feels. If you encounter an area of tension or discomfort, acknowledge it before moving on.

Once you've finished the scan, take a moment and pull your findings together. Was it an overall positive or negative experience? Did you notice any stress on your body? Did you have any negativity? Are there areas you need to adjust? Body scans are a great way to get in touch with our physical being. The more familiar we are with our body, the greater the chance we can interrupt its typical patterns and exert mindful change over it.

Set a timer for five minutes and complete a body scan meditation from the previous page.

....

1. Did you find the exercise easy or difficult? Why?

2. Did any areas stand out as having more tension than others during your body scan? Which areas?

3. Once you noticed the tension and moved on from that area, did anything happen? Did the tension hold on tight or did it disappear as you moved away from it?

4. Were there any areas that were completely relaxed?

5. What did you learn from this exercise?

....

We often have areas of our bodies that are more affected by stress than others. Do you have an area that is painful or tight when you're under stress? Spend a few moments simply drawing your attention to this area and letting it linger there. Remember to be completely unbiased in your focus; you're simply observing the area. What was your experience? Did the pain lessen, or did it seem to expand?

....

What does your body feel like when you experience joy? What about sadness? How does emotion affect your physicality?

Sit with your feet planted on the floor, and spend a few moments feeling the effects of gravity on your body. Trace all of the areas in which you can feel the pressure of your chair and floor on your body with your mind. Were there any areas in which the pressure was more, or less? Was it evenly distributed or unbalanced?

Our hands are often an area that carries an incredible amount of tension, but because we use them frequently, we don't notice it. Lay your hands on the table in front of you and close your eyes. Relax the muscles and draw your attention to the palms of your hands. Is there any tension that you can feel? Now, think about the root of that tension. Is there anything in your brain that could be affecting your body today?

Complete another body scan meditation, even if it's only for a few moments. Was this different from your first body scan? Were the areas of tension and comfort the same or different?

....

How do you feel about your body? Write ten

positive things you love about your body.

Pick an obscure area of the body, an area that typically doesn't receive much attention in our daily lives. Elbows, ankles, and ears are great starting points. Draw your focus to one of these areas and observe it for an emotional quality. Which area did you pick? What emotions are tied to that area?

Do you have a body part that you're not particularly fond of? Think about that area. Now practice loving-kindness. Forgive yourself for your perceived imperfections. How does that positive self-talk feel?

When doing a routine task, make note of how your body is moving. Tune in to your movements. Feel your muscles flex and bones shift. What have you learned about your body and its power?

....

Go on a mindful walk in nature. Take note of how your body feels moving outside. Do you feel more relaxed in the open space? How does your body relate to its surroundings?

For this prompt, please use the opposite of your dominant hand. It will look terrible, and that's okay! Pick up a writing utensil and write something—anything—on a page for one minute. How does that feel? Think about the muscles you're using. Do you sense any discomfort, tension?

We occasionally shoulder more weight and stress from those around us. Particularly empathetic people can draw this weight onto their own shoulders and help others. What are some signs that you are shouldering the burden for others? Does it manifest in physical stress? Emotional?

....

Meditation

Meditation is an integral part of mindfulness. Think about meditation as going to the gym for your emotional and mental health. A little bit here and there is great, but overall, consistency is key, and the longer you do it, the healthier you will be!

There are many different ways to meditate. There's mindful breathing and body scans. You can download meditation apps or simply spend an uninterrupted minute of focus on an object or feeling. Each of these techniques can be used separately or in sequence during the same session, gently moving your focus from your breath to your body and back again.

How long should you meditate for at a time? Only spend as long as you feel comfortable and as long as it's pleasant. If you feel comfortable to push yourself a little further, you can increase your meditation time, but we should stress that meditation should be a pleasant experience. So, if you're feeling exhausted or emotionally tired after your practice, find a new way to approach meditation. Switch it up!

NEW TECHNIQUE: MINDFUL BREATHING

This technique is simple in that it is short and you have the ability to practice at any time! It only requires your breath. Sit however is comfortable to you. Take several moments to ensure that you're comfortable and relatively undisturbed. Take a few deep breaths and close your eyes, allowing your breath to return to its natural rhythm. You will be able to feel the air entering past your nostrils as you breathe. You may focus on this feeling, or the feeling of your chest and stomach expanding with each breath.

Gently draw your attention to one of these feelings and settle it there. You will occasionally be distracted by a pop of unwanted thought or emotional response. This is perfectly normal. When you've noticed that your attention has strayed from your breath, gently draw your attention back to its focus. As your practice progresses, you'll begin to be distracted less and less. All you're looking for is one good breath. Do not push yourself for too long too early into your practice. Start with one minute and progress from there as you feel more and more comfortable with the exercise.

Complete a ten-minute session of the mindful breathing technique above, then answer the following questions.

....

1. What does meditation mean to you? Have you practiced some form of meditation before? What are your wellness goals?

2. Did you struggle to find your breath? Where did you feel it? Did you notice a change in your breathing pattern or pace?

3. What was the emotional state of the mind today? Was it restless, or did you find it easy to follow the breath?

4. Were there any thoughts that were harder to acknowledge and move past?

....

You have now been practicing mindfulness for some time now, what are your reasons for learning meditation and mindfulness? Revisit the answers that you gave previously in the workbook. Have they changed? How?

....

Often throughout the day, we can experience intrusive thoughts that are tough to shake. Make a list of ten things that have constantly been on your mind. Get them out on the page. Now take stock of this list, acknowledge these thoughts and the power they hold, and move past them.

Often the future is a source of anxiety for people.
Is this true with you? Think about where your
anxiety stems from. What's the main source?

....

Think of a time when you were totally serene. When was it? What factors were influencing you in that moment? Can you re-create that peace?

Complete a session of mindful breathing. What was the emotional quality of the mind today? Was it frantic or peaceful? Remember that neither is better than the other and that all emotions are valid and important.

....

Take a few moments to focus on your breath. Was focusing difficult? If it was, it will get easier with time. What about the pace of your breathing today, was it fast and abrupt, or slow and measured?

....

We often occupy many different roles in our lives, boss, employee, spouse, partner, friend—and we shift between them easily. What is your primary role right now? How does it affect others? Take sixty seconds and think about your roles in the world. How do you move between them?

Our emotional qualities can often change drastically throughout the day, and that's okay. Is there a time when you feel the most grounded and strong? When is that?

. . . .

Take a few moments to imagine your perfect day, from beginning to end. Imagine what meals you eat and your perfect mindfulness or meditation practice. Write it down here.

There are many values that make up our guiding compass in life. What are a few that are most important to you?

Glance back at any of your previous entries throughout the workbook so far. Have you noticed any positive changes from your practice? If so, write them below.

....

What is one of your personal goals right now? Close

your eyes for a few moments and vividly visualize

achieving this goal. How does this make you feel? What

can you do to take a step toward this goal today?

....

Self-Love

Our self-image is a source of many of our positive and negative thought patterns. When things become challenging, it is easy to submit to a cycle of blame instead of congratulating ourselves for all that we can and have achieved. We are often our hardest critics, holding ourselves to impossibly high standards and doling out self-reprimands for every perceived slight or failure. Mindfulness is a path out of those negative patterns. When we're mindful and present in our experiences, we're able to learn compassionate responses and cultivate an attitude of compassion.

Our minds, perhaps over years of negative training and reinforcement, have learned that the safest way to move through the world is to assume that we are the problem. That we are responsible for the bad moods or negative feelings of others. This is simply wrong. These thoughts defeat us before we've even begun. Before we assume responsibility for all of our negative experiences, we must be absolutely certain that we are the cause of them. We must inspect the circumstances and events of our lives and practice ownership, forgiveness, and compassion. The only way to break out of this cycle is to practice mindful self-love.

What does this process of self-love look like? It often begins with loving-kindness and compassion toward the self and all those around us. We must learn to forgive ourselves for making errors and underperforming. Then, when our default turns from blame to self-love, we develop a positive mentality that influences the world around us.

NEW TECHNIQUE: SELF-LOVE MEDITATION

Sit in a comfortable space without distraction. Begin by taking several deep breaths in through the nose and out through the mouth. Pay attention to the feeling of the breath, much like in the mindful breathing exercise. For a few moments, keep your awareness on the breath.

Now, let your awareness settle on your sense of self. It may help to imagine yourself in a mirror. First, you must forgive yourself for previous self-criticisms and conflicts. These are common, but you must actively forgive yourself for the guilt and stress that you may have caused yourself. Spend a few moments thinking of yourself with total forgiveness. Think about the times when you believed you failed. Think about your sense of self, your self-criticisms and critiques. Forgive it all. Now shift your focus to a place of gratitude. You must thank yourself for getting to where you are in life. Thank yourself for all the successes you've had and you will have. And finally, focus on the feeling of love, the culmination of all these emotions. Spend a few moments feeling the warmth of your own self-love. It may help to imagine saying "I love you" to your mirror image. Attempt to wrap yourself in this emotion, until the end of your practice.

Complete a five-minute session of the self-love meditation
and then answer the following questions.

....

1. Was there an instance or self-critique that was particularly difficult to dismiss? Why do you think you were holding on to that
criticism?

2. We occasionally forget that we have people on our side. Think of
a few of them now. How would they try to convince you to love
yourself?

3. What was the overall emotion you felt after the meditation? Did
you feel any relief from the practice?

....

What are some of your favorite traits? Make a
list of ten traits you love about yourself.

If you had to pick a personality trait or habit you wanted to cultivate, what would it be? How can you begin to cultivate that habit or trait today?

....

Think of a time when you've practiced forgiveness. Describe that time. Where was that forgiveness directed? What did it feel like?

Now, think about a time where you were at fault for something. Write about that experience. How would it feel to have your own forgiveness? Others' forgiveness?

Is there a time when you were surprised by your feelings or actions? Write about that situation. What were your perceived thought patterns, and how did you disrupt them?

What are some of the things you're really great at?

Make a list of all the areas where you excel.

. . . .

What gives you strength? What makes you feel proud?

What is something you should forgive yourself
for but you haven't yet? Why not? Try not to be
judgmental, instead, simply acknowledge the situation
and your part in it. How does forgiveness feel?

....

Name three people who inspire you. What
traits do they possess that you respect?

Name three things someone else loves about you. You can either guess or actually ask them for extra points!

. . . .

When are you most self-confident? Why? What does it feel like to be in those situations?

Complete another session of self-love meditation.

Was it easier than last time? Why or why not?

....

Mindful Self-Care

Are you the friend everyone goes to with their problems? An ever-present shoulder to cry on? Every conversation adding another sandbag to your shoulders? If you find yourself more and more on others' needs instead of your own, you may be on the brink of compassion fatigue. That's where self-care can come in.

Before we can improve on our mindfulness practice, and in other areas of our lives, we must first understand our own needs and see to our personal self-care. During our hectic lives, we rarely take the time to assess and understand what keeps us going and how to continue to fuel the machine. We struggle to analyze our habits and discern what is truly serving us. Mindfulness helps us recognize how and why we need to treat ourselves better.

Much like on a plane, it is necessary to put our masks on before we help others. Before we can succeed in our various roles, we need to understand how to fulfill our sense of self.

Self-care is how we can nurture our mental, emotional, and physical needs.

One thing to note is that self-care is not selfish or self-fulfilling. Taking care of yourself only expands your ability to help and support others, but you need to dedicate the time. Imagine you have a well of love and care that you can give to the people around you. The more you tend your well, the more you can share with those in your life. Taking care of yourself puts you in the position to help those around you without reservation.

Make a list of all your favorite self-care practices. Consider your sleep habits, your diet, your mindfulness, and your hobbies. Whenever you feel that your self-care routines/ requirements could use some fine-tuning, or adjustments, return to this list and ensure you're meeting all of your needs.

Take stock of your current self-care situation. What does your self-care look like? Where can you improve? What do you wish you could incorporate into your self-care?

....

What does self-care mean to you? Why do you think
it's important to your mindfulness journey?

What is a self-care technique you've always wanted to
try but never have? What is holding you back?

....

Make a list of the little victories you've experienced in the past month. How can you reward yourself for these experiences?

Have you ever felt guilt for engaging in self-care? Why? Redirect that feeling of guilt and forgive yourself for that criticism. Embrace self-care as an important facet of your wellness. How does that feel?

....

Think of an activity that makes you blissfully happy.
How can we make time to do that activity this
week? What does your ideal day look like?

....

What is something nice that you've done for
yourself lately? How did that make you feel?

Think about a day of uninterrupted self-care. What emotions do you experience? What thought patterns do you notice? Are they positive, negative, or a mix? Take a mindful look and register these experiences. What do they say about your relationship with self-care?

Identify five emotions you experienced today. Of those five emotions, which was the hardest to deal with? Why? What self-care activity would help manage that emotion?

....

Are there any habits or activities that soothe you after a long day? What are they? Make a list of your favorite relaxation techniques.

Revisit one bad thing that happened to you this week.
Now, rewrite it so it has a positive lesson. How does
this mindfulness technique tie in to your self-care?

....

Describe what it feels like when nothing seems to be going your way. How do your mind and body respond? Now, describe what it feels like when everything is going your way. How can you manifest that positivity and re-create those feel-good moments?

Gratitude

Gratitude is perhaps the most powerful healing tool we have in our mindfulness belt. Gratitude has an intense connection to the present state, and as mindfulness practitioners, we should always strive to be present and grateful for each moment. When we feel gratitude, we cannot be thinking of future worries or past regrets. We can only be thankful for what we have in the now.

Aside from a regular meditation and mindfulness practice, regularly experiencing gratitude is key to cultivating a healthy and peaceful mind.

"Count your blessings" is a very real and accurate aphorism. It is very difficult to be negative when we're actively seeking out our gifts and blessings. Gratitude need not apply only to the physical things around us. Yes, we can experience gratitude for the roof over our head and the food we eat, but we can also be grateful for the situations we find ourselves in—even the difficult ones. We can be thankful that we are being tested and that we are learning from our circumstances. We can be appreciative of a difficult situation that has proven how strong we can be.

Gratitude is one of the most profound and positive ways we can relate to the world around us. So why is it so hard to practice gratitude in our daily lives? Often, we simply overlook our everyday blessings. We live in the future, always pushing for the next thing. Through mindfulness, we can once again step back, out of the constant stream of thoughts, and notice the things we are grateful for.

NEW TECHNIQUE: GRATITUDE PRACTICE

Sit in an area where you'll be undisturbed and comfortable. Take a few deep breaths, feeling the air fill your lungs. Pick three experiences you are grateful for. They can be as minor as your favorite book or as significant as your access to clean water. You can be grateful for a trying situation, a loving friend, anything that you feel is a blessing in your life. Bring your focus to your first example. Feel the emotion of gratitude welling up within your chest. Feel your thankfulness for it. Imagine life without it, and thank the situation for presenting itself in your life. Repeat this process with your remaining two objects.

Think about all the things you're grateful for. Fill this page with your gratitude, from the big to the small. Refer back during trying times to help gain some perspective.

What is a difficult experience or trying time you've
endured that you're now thankful for? Describe
that situation and how it impacted your life.

Make a list of the things that made you smile this week. Meditate on those good moments. How do they make you feel?

Is there a type of food you're particularly grateful

for? A guilty pleasure or a daily ritual?

What projects or goals have you finished lately? What skills did you need to complete those tasks? How can you thank yourself for the achievements?

....

Describe a place where you feel safe. Imagine
yourself in that space. How does it make you feel?
Why do you think it has that effect on you?

....

What risk are you most grateful for taking? How did
that risk impact your life? What did you learn?

Think of a time when you were flexible. How did this benefit you? Allow yourself to feel thankful of your past self.

Have you ever had a confrontation that you're thankful you had? Why? What did that experience teach you?

....

Make a list of ten things you're thankful for today. Throughout the week, meditate on your list. How did it make you feel?

Who are some people in your life who you are thankful for?

How can you let them know what they mean to you?

....

Make a list of five affirmations you can repeat to
yourself to express your gratitude. During your
mindfulness practice, focus on those affirmations.

Make a list of things you want to manifest. What tools do you already have to bring these experiences into your life?

Mindful Emotions

During our meditative practice, we will encounter many emotions that we have never taken the time to fully understand. As we focus on our breath and our body, emotions and thoughts will inevitably intrude. This is always to be expected. However, now we have an opportunity to better understand our emotional landscapes and become conscious of them, and their triggers, as they occur throughout our days.

As we learn to understand and feel our own emotions more productively, we open ourselves up to the opportunity to be more in tune with others. This practice of feeling and understanding the forms of our own emotions will let us better recognize the same emotions and feelings in others. We all handle emotions differently, but we all feel these emotions in some form or other. We must handle our own emotional baggage before we can properly assess and react to the emotions around us.

In life, we can't expect everyone to react to their emotions the same. We must recognize that other people lead emotionally rich lives, just like ours. They are full of joy, sadness, anger, and insecurity. However, through mindfulness, we can gain self-awareness and learn to express our own emotions so that we can handle others with empathy and respect.

Being mindful of our evolving emotional landscapes is a great way to foster interpersonal relationships and create lasting connections.

NEW TECHNIQUE: 30-SECOND LOVING-KINDNESS MEDITATION

This technique is easiest when in a public space or otherwise near people. Settle yourself in a chair or stand in a relaxed position with your eyes open. Take a few deep breaths. Pick a person in your line of sight. They can be someone you know well or a stranger. Imagine sending them thoughts and feelings of warmth and comfort. Send them wishes for their safety and success. Honestly hope that this person discovers happiness in all that they do. Feel these emotions fill you as you focus on their emotional landscape. Remember, if you get distracted by a different thought or feeling, gently return your focus to your loving-kindness subject. Do this for sixty seconds. Take several deep breaths, and open your eyes.

The loving-kindness meditation can be completed at any time, with any person, and fosters a sense of connectedness and empathy. Pick someone who is emotionally close to you, and complete a minute of loving-kindness meditation, then answer the following questions.

1. What did your emotional landscape look like before the meditation? How did you feel after completing it?

2. If you could give this person any message right now, what would it be?

3. How do you think this exercise would change if you picked someone you have had negative emotional experiences with?

Take stock of your current emotional landscape. What does it look like? Parse out the individual feelings and put them on the page.

....

Has there been a time when you understood someone's emotional state well? Describe what that felt like. How did you empathize with that person?

· ·

How do you express anger? How do you express joy?

Describe a time when you've experienced a negative
emotion. How did you heal from that situation?
What did you learn about that emotion?

Do you find it difficult to understand how people are feeling? Why or why not?

....

Just like our own emotions, we must openly accept the emotions of others. List five ways you can better understand or acknowledge others' emotions.

. . . .

Emotions are rarely easy to perfectly define. Pick one of your prominent emotions from the past month. How would you contextualize it? What shape does it take?

....

How do you tend to manage your emotions? Are they easily expressed, or do you often shutter them away?

How does it feel to talk about your emotional landscape with a close friend? With a stranger? Describe that feeling. Sit with it for a moment and note if you have a body reaction to the memory.

Has there been an emotion recently that you've had a hard time accepting and noting? One that constantly pulls you out of the present? Which emotion is it? Why does it have this power over you?

....

How do other people impact your emotions? How much power do they wield over your feelings?

....

What are some of the strong emotions you've experienced recently? List them across the page and add an arrow pointing up for a positive emotion or an arrow pointing down for a negative emotion. What does your roller coaster look like?

Mindful Relationships

Our lives are composed of countless relationships. Whether they be tenuous acquaintances, close friends, or somewhere in between, our social structure is one of the most important facets of our culture. Our relationships with friends, family, and society in general drastically affect our mental and emotional sates.

Our relationships can be the source of great love and joy, as well as pain and suffering. We all wish to be seen, heard, and understood, and the conflicts in our relationships often stem from one of these needs not being met. Mindfulness can help us work on these issues.

Our mindful concepts of living in the present applies to not only our breath but our relationships as well. Instead of recognizing their true nature, or how people behave, we often create pictures of them in our heads. We develop images based on how we want people to act. This attachment often conflicts with how they *do* act, causing friction between our vision and reality.

Bringing mindfulness into our relationships can have amazing benefits. We can foster higher-quality relationships with less conflict. When we are mindful of our own emotions and deal with ourselves and others with self-awareness and empathy, lines that previously would have been crossed remain open and communicative.

Our mindfulness also lowers our emotional reactivity. It's easier to handle a perceived slight from a partner or friend when we focus on our reaction in the present and unpack the moment with compassion and presence.

Overall, as our capacity for empathy grows, our interactions become more compassionate and ultimately more productive. Happy, mindful people make better partners, friends, coworkers, and employers!

Take a few minutes to write down several of the relationships that are most important to you. For each of them, answer the following questions.

....

1. Why is this relationship important to you?
2. How does this relationship make you feel?
3. How would you feel if this relationship ended?
4. Do you have any plans for where you'd like this relationship to go?
5. Unpack a miscommunication you've had in this relationship. What was the root of that miscommunication?

....

What relationships are you most thankful for right now? Why?

What relationship in your life, past or present, has affected you the most? Why do you think that person had an impact? Describe the emotional quality of that relationship.

. . . .

Is there a relationship that you need to adjust or reassess?

What emotions do you tend to foster around that person?

Is there a relationship that you want to improve specifically?

Who is it? How do you plan to strengthen this connection?

. . . .

Describe how you listen. Do you think you can improve your listening skills? How?

Think of some interactions you've had recently. Were they productive? Were they positive and compassionate? If not, what will you do differently in the future?

....

Are you properly communicating your needs and wants
to those closest to you in your life? Why can that be
difficult? Unpack some of the emotions that are tied
up with that level of openness and honesty.

....

What is your most positive or joyous relationship?

How can you spend more time with that person?

What do boundaries mean to you? Why are they important? Do you have solid relationship boundaries in your life?

What are your core values and priorities right now?

Do they align with your current relationships?

Describe a conflict that you've had to overcome with someone in your life. How did the conflict arise? How do you typically handle interpersonal conflict?

How do you think the people around you would describe you? Free write in the space below.

How to Have a Mindful Morning

GET GOOD SLEEP

The foundation of a mindful morning starts with quality sleep. If we hope to succeed in having a mindful morning, we cannot be waking up to a blaring alarm, bleary eyed and with a fogged brain. Plan ahead and ensure you're setting aside enough time to get full, restful sleep. Turn off devices before you hit the hay. Practice some mindful breathing techniques or other meditation to unwind after a long day. Do what you need to do to leave you well rested and ready for the morning to arrive.

YOUR PHONE AND EMAIL CAN WAIT

For many of us, the first thing we do when we wake in the morning is roll over and begin scrolling through our email or social media. This is a terrible habit. As soon as we wake, we bombard ourselves with all the messages on electronic devices—incurring stress and taking us out of the present. Instead, take the time normally spent scrolling to allow yourself to wake up gently. Be present as you stretch your limbs, open your eyes, and greet the day.

DON'T RUSH

Our morning routines typically take the same amount of time day in and day out. Clock that routine and give yourself an extra twenty minutes to relax and greet the day. Instead of rapid-fire dressing and rushing out the door, set your alarm earlier and sit quietly with your thoughts. Prepare yourself to take on the day's challenges and begin with a healthy, mindful morning.

COMPLETE YOUR MEDITATION OR MINDFULNESS JOURNALING

Perhaps one of the most important parts of your morning routine should be writing in this workbook or one like it! Often when we wake up in the morning, we're in a prime creative space.

That makes the mornings an excellent time to do our meditative practice. Even five minutes of mindful breathing can have a profound effect on the rest of our day. If you must pick only one of the above recommendations for your mornings, this is by far the only choice. Journaling and meditating in the morning will set a successful mindful tone for the rest of your day.

How to Have a Mindful Day

GRATITUDE FIRST

Gratitude is one of the easiest ways to remain mindful throughout the day. It doesn't require any special techniques or any time at all. We must simply recognize when we can be thankful and allow ourselves that emotion. If you're having trouble remembering to be grateful, set yourself a small alarm or timer on your phone that will remind you to do so. Take those few moments to think of several things that you're grateful for.

TAKE A WALK

Many of us often spend too much time sitting inside. This sedentary lifestyle drastically shortens our lifespan, and a stagnant lifestyle can affect our thought patterns. Often, it's helpful, especially in creative pursuits, to get up and move around. You can use a simple walk to the bathroom at work, or a walking commute, to add a little bit of mindfulness to your day.

Begin by taking a few deep breaths and a step. You should

be aware of all the muscles that must move and contract to lift your foot off the ground and place it ahead of you. Make every movement deliberate. After a few steps, you're able to shift your focus from the actual movements to the rhythm of your feet on the ground. Keep your focus there as you move throughout the world. If you find yourself getting distracted, gently draw your attention back to the rhythm of your feet.

ONE GOOD BREATH

Part of the beauty of a mindfulness practice is that we can take a few moments whenever possible and practice. We may not always *believe* that we have that ability, but we do! Remember, you're often only looking for one good breath. One breath where you are completely focused on the present. Once you've achieved your breath, you can return to your tasks.

How to Have a Mindful Night

ADJUST YOUR SETTING

Your nighttime routine should start with putting your room and your space in order. Do any of the small cleaning tasks that may be nagging at you. Pay special attention to the areas where you're going to prepare for bed. You want the area you're in to reflect the type of mindset you want as you finish your day. Don't tidy up if you don't want to! "In order" doesn't necessarily mean "clean." It just means whatever you're most comfortable in.

Set the mood of the evening by lighting candles and turning on some soft music. Dim the lights in preparation for sleep and disconnect from devices. All of these things should result in a space that feels peaceful and calm.

DAILY REVIEW

An excellent addition to your night routine is a daily review of the day.

This process can be as simple as curling up in bed with a mug of caffeine-free tea and unpacking all the things that happened during the day. You can keep the day's experiences in your mind, acknowledge their presence, and dismiss them as you prepare for a new day ahead.

Take the time to think about how you handled certain situations. Were your interactions with others compassionate? Were you self-aware today? Was your practice difficult or easy? What can you potentially improve on tomorrow? Spend a few minutes each night either writing these questions down or just mentally reviewing them in your head.

MINDFUL BREATHING

Alongside your journaling, it can be beneficial to include another round of mindful breathing before you head to sleep. Do not do this in your bed! Your bed should only be associated with actual sleeping. We want to calm the mind with our mindful breathing meditation, not put it directly to sleep!

Take a few moments to close your eyes and focus your attention on your breath. Feel the sensation of the air passing through your nostrils and filling your lungs. Breathe out through your mouth. Feel your lungs expand with air and your shoulders rise with it. Focus on the sensation and let everything else ease away.

Conclusion

Like any new skill, mindfulness requires consistent practice, and now that you've reached the end of this workbook, you're ready to fully embrace your new mindfulness journey. With your newfound tools and a dedicated routine underway, you now have what you need to integrate mindfulness in your day-to-day life. While you go, feel free to revisit this workbook at any time. With each pass, you'll learn something new about your life, your mental health, and yourself. All it takes is one minute a day to achieve a more peaceful, mindful life.